Notness

Selected Writings 7

RICHARD BERENGARTEN was born in London in 1943, into a family of musicians. He has lived in Italy, Greece, the USA and former Yugoslavia. His perspectives as a poet combine English, French, Mediterranean, Jewish, Slavic, American and Oriental influences.

Under the name RICHARD BURNS, he has published more than 25 books. In the 1970s, he founded and ran the international Cambridge Poetry Festival. In the UK he has received the Eric Gregory Award, the Wingate-Jewish Quarterly Award for Poetry, the Keats Poetry Prize, and the Yeats Club Prize. In Serbia, he has received the international Morava Charter Poetry Prize and the Great Lesson Award, and in Macedonia, the Manada Prize. He has been Writer-in-Residence at the international Eliot-Dante Colloquium in Florence, Arts Council Writer-in-Residence at the Victoria Centre in Gravesend, Royal Literary Fund Fellow at Newnham College, Cambridge, and a Royal Literary Fund Project Fellow. He has been Visiting Associate Professor at the University of Notre Dame and British Council Lecturer in Belgrade, first at the Centre for Foreign Languages and then at the Philological Faculty. He is a Fellow of the English Association, a Bye-Fellow at Downing College, Cambridge, and Praeceptor at Corpus Christi College, Cambridge. His poems have been translated into more than 90 languages.

Notness

Metaphysical Sonnets

RICHARD BERENGARTEN

Shearsman Books

This edition published in the United Kingdom in 2015
by Shearsman Books Ltd
50 Westons Hill Drive
Emersons Green
BRISTOL
BS16 7DF

Shearsman Books Ltd Registered Office
30–31 St. James Place, Mangotsfield, Bristol BS16 9JB
(this address not for correspondence)

www.shearsman.com

ISBN 978-1-84861-381-2

For Barrie and Patricia Irving

He sat and expounded to them: The *Shekhinah* is below as it is above. And what is this *Shekhinah*? Let us say that it is the light that has emanated from the Primal Light...

SEFER HA BAHIR

And now the moment. Such a moment is unique. It is, of course, brief and temporal, as moments are, ephemeral, as moments are, passed, as moments are, in the next moment, and yet it is decisive, and yet it is filled with eternity. Such a moment must have a special name. Let us call it the fullness of time.

SØREN KIERKEGAARD

When I seek for the ultimate reasons of mechanicalism and the laws of motion I am surprised to discover that they are not to be found in mathematics and that we must turn to metaphysics.

G. W. LEIBNIZ

I believe that if one takes Einstein's general relativity seriously, one must allow for the possibility that spacetime ties itself in knots and that information gets lost in the folds.

STEPHEN HAWKING

Neither a pure flow nor pure present moments make any coherent sense. And yet in music we hear this impossible reconciliation. To believe the evidence of our ears is therefore to deny nihilism.

CATHERINE PICKSTOCK

Enlarge art?
No. On the contrary, take art with you into your innermost narrowness. And set yourself free.

PAUL CELAN

Contents

Dwelling
~ for the *Shekhinah*

Moon over sea

Times when joy's so full I feel I could burst –
when in fact *I* does burst: explodes in thous-
ands of connecting splinters, the way those
moonflecks spill and ripple tide-wide waves. Best
then never swell to encompass this beast
(many-faced) identity. Rather with these
phantasms, let all fail, flake, fly. Since all withers
eventually, why flinch, fluster, flail, wail, boast?
Catch joys rather in their moments of disappearing
into unthinking, únthought, thought's entire
notness – past fellow feeling, past fearing
of falling apart, past loss, past past desire –
and never mind their melting or those searing
yellow and blue flames vaulting in black fire.

Home

Gift to my heart, my soul's hostess and home,
interior, bless'd before time ever was,
before *wherefores* and *whys*, before *because*,
temple of skies with starred or clouded dome,
treasure so quickly gone I cannot wait
when loss sets in with its cold stony grin
and occupies all space that's left within –
useless I call, *Gone, gone,* but call too late
through absence to scry miserable fate.
Yet home is this and you whatever this
in presence proffers to my innerness –
you guest, you gust of wind, you swinging gate –
with you and this now how could I not still
be sure that I belonged in miracle?

Siesta

Where does your skin, or mine, begin or end?
Stilled in the wake of storms we woke and spurred,
my borders, lying next to yours, float blurred
among these waves we failed to tire or spend.
Through hand-clasp, elbow-crook, hip-fold, knee-bend,
you wrapped me in you as our passion stirred
(and through each other's passions, more incurred).
And still our bodies merge. Our beings blend.
What shall be said then (rich loss? faint *tristesse?*)
when what we know is this calm tenderness?
How sudden separation is – and yet
now, as we sleep-wake, cool net curtains let
kind breeze in from this sunny afternoon.
Relishing this, we'll shower, go out soon.

Night bathing, Aegean

On the beach we strip, watching pin-eyed ships
flicker through dark. Nor shall we wait to hide
our nakedness, but running, cast aside
warm sun-bronzed skins of daylight's swimming dips.
Now you are all moons, ovals in ellipse
orbiting me. Pale, glistening, purified,
slow we come in to land, lapped by the tide –
to suck out salt from *Aphrodite's* lips.
Listen, love, to the waves. Hump-backed, they're hauling
nets of black light around the flanks of Greece.
A creaking-timbered moon, full sailed, is trawling
this August night for shooting stars, its fleece,
while, curled up in their wake, someone lies calling
small white cries, like a seagull, for release.

Soul of my soul

Soul of my soul, my soul's inner retreat
and nucleus, you still innermost space
that occupy no space yet light her face
in glance of recognition when we meet –
you now as commonplace on way or street
as stone but quite untouchable in place
being her possessionless pure grace
and miracle – perfectly incomplete
for being instantaneous, lacking name,
beginningless, unpassing, without end –
movement through leaves, sensed radiance and sheen
in all things, yet yourself always unseen –
in me be present yet and through me send
breath, spirit, ghost, and ecstasy of flame.

Though numbed by passing

Though numbed by passing and surpassing fear
and bound to *being* on this trembling ground
I stand on all the while you spin me round
the axis of a passion or a year,
giddied I listen, having no choice but hear
your song composed of noteless silent sound,
as if unhemmed, and your whole nature crowned
in glints, caught up in waves, now blurred, now near.
Over the waters, shimmering, a face
I've half thought yours appears to smile and call
and back I call, Time, come, I am the space
you long to lodge in, and take over all
its darkest corners from, and light in grace,
unsure if still I stumble, rise or fall.

True to your absence, glory

Is glory in the residue, mere evidence,
in shining track, in afterglow, in spoor?
Being too poor to meet you in your residence
I plead with glory, greet me at your door,
fully resplendent, present, now, revealed
hostlike to your *main tenant* in this space.
But you come always partially concealed
in mist, with indistinctly profiled face
hanging in haze, ghostlike. We shall remain
true to your absence, glory, seeing you are
bright only as a long exploded star,
a mote in darkness, spreading like a stain,
present but in the shrinking and the swelling,
their course in timespace, and their aftertelling.

Insomniac presence

To wake up, and to be – being wide awake –
are different. The first calls *dawn, arising*,
a first sun pouring light across the lake,
brilliance for seeing through, not analysing.
Night, sinking fast, a drowning wreck capsizing
under the ghosthood of its foamless wake,
gives way, itself away, all compromising,
and brittle vials of dark expand and break.
But I dream of a being that can't sleep
whose constant state is steadily aware
of all that is and can be, anywhere.
Insomniac presence, missing you, I weep,
denied in thought-knots as I watch and keep
calling for you, on you, who are not there.

Radiance, palpable

Time is a chance we cannot choose but take.
Outside it, from this world at least, the odds
are nought to zero. Push our luck and break
rank from all other runners, not being gods?
If we'd been brought to life through play or mime
into some scarcely recognizable vast
non-time, un-time, anterior to time,
in which the very pastness of the past
had turned (or has, or even will have turned)
into radiance, palpable – to a glory
so overspilling presence that the burned
disintegrating day-ends of our story
dissolved – then, might we really take our chance
to be, outside of being, in that radiance?

This scintillating night

This scintillating night is filled with subtlest
variations of light. They interlace
then cancel, like expressions on a face,
yours, in this case. How curiously we're blessed,
witnessing this, as if being called, addressed
directly, on this huge-dimensioned base
by all the puzzling splendour of time-space
that placement and momentum might attest.
Let us be true, then, to each other's love
though what we'd track in passing can't be touched –
scarcely discerned – in those far heights above,
and though we pass like shoals of arrows clutched
by wind in soaring flight and lightning-flecked
in sentient transience here all things connect.

Bitter Loving

She had to leave

She had to leave. There was no point in trying
to be herself, and love him, since the two
devotions would not match, and to be true
to one of them meant she must kill the other.
She knew it in her marrow. Her own mother
could be no closer to her than was he.
But then, her mother-death had left her free
to live the life she had been simply dying.
She knew she hurt him, and she suffered guilt
for moving on, as though his corpse, all bloody,
still occupied each cell of her soul-body,
as if she'd thrust a blade in, to the hilt.
Instead of giving him her life, she'd live
away from him, and hope he would forgive.

To himself

Deep in his heart, black wounds he dare not show.
He's weary, cursed, a being in distress,
that sparkle in the eyes, that starry brow –
as good as dead. All paths are emptiness.
Death is his track in every step he takes,
Death, in his belly and in every breath,
Death is his drink and daily bread he breaks,
in expectation and attainment, Death.
What use desire, its hope without a goal
or lust's quick flicker, when there's neither cure
nor rest, in breath or heartbeat, for his soul,
and though his loves are beautiful and pure
like faded perfume in a broken bowl
none of his babbling larksong can endure?

after the Croatian of Tin Ujević

Because she left him

Because she left him, now he can't avoid
his terror of collapsing – so far into
himself, he fears his fall will plunge him through
his bowels, into non-being, where, in a void
of spaceless nothingness, to be destroyed
is certain. He thinks now she merely 'toyed
with his affections', recalling very clearly
ways that her eyes had darlinged him, too dearly.
Nor had he dreamt that she might leave him, who
had once instilled an unsuspecting joy.
He wanted her to succour him right through
his suffering, as though he were a boy.
She could not, would not do that. He must wake
up from his mother-making, or else break.

The Gulf

The Gulf – whole oceans scaled over his head
and gold fish fashioned out of crystallites.
He asks where Madam Moonlight's lain abed
and blue horizons haze blue mountain heights.
His dawn is spiked with delicate clear dread,
thought's needles – piercing, lucid – snap and freeze,
no scales or spirals raise him in their stead
nor mirrorings of rocked realities.
His heart's a zone unfathomed, fertile, deep,
beneath whose leaden sky he breaks and sinks
while life, a seagull, soars over his head.
Aye, well-fed woman, easy, full of bread,
thought's rhythms broke our last connecting links,
but how my heart and pulse beat, beat and leap.

after the Croatian of Tin Ujević

Anniversary

She phoned and told him that two rats were playing
outside the call box. They were 'sweet', she said.
Numbed, he could hardly hear what she was saying
and wished that she'd come back, or he were dead.
Shrill whistlings in his ear, blasts of despair,
deafened him, and his back ached. He regressed
to whining, infant-like, and didn't care.
The doctor called him 'clinically depressed',
suffering from 'pathological grief',
and needing medication. Was the best way
forward then backwards? How to find relief
or at least rest? If he had any say
in futures, he would beg her on his knees
back home to cure him. No hope. What use? *Please?*

Leave me the chasms

Leave me the chasms, the chaos, leave the gulf,
leave nettle poison, rags. Take everything.
I'll be a mountain cave, live like a wolf
or crazed wild man, eyes full of suffering,
who cannot learn what love has always claimed
but longs to find it, unsheathed from the clasp
of someone who owns nothing, naked, maimed:
to give all for a dream beyond his grasp,
to die in peace, yet drink life's bitterness,
to sieve pure song, full throated, out of thunder,
to sound the depths of woman's innerness,
then perish on full lips, flesh ripped asunder,
yet not be bound to earth by bony time,
a prisoner gripped by his petty crime.

after the Serbian of Oskar Davičo

These stubs of pain

These stubs of pain have shrivelled, since your fire
has burned them out and what was left, their ash,
scattered on windswept water, and desire
blistered on the flickering of an eyelash,
smudged, crumbled and dispersed – except for *this*.
Whatever self your substance might allow
has so unravelled, past analysis,
that what *I* was no longer matters now.
So, skittering, feeble, pitter-pattering heart,
although you seem past breaking, still you'll beat
on, on, tímekeeping for the voiceless part
that heralds this – an *I* that can't retreat
to habitats of longing, well entrained
by those on whom your love has never rained.

Inner calmer

I *dream-sleep-wake*. I dream I wake asleep.
I ask my calmer, lest I overleap.
'What fallow ploughfield will you let me keep?'
He's cunning, will not answer, being too deep,
but grins back and says nothing, stays opaque.
I tell him, 'Truth's transparent. Yours is fake.'
I *wake-dream-sleep*. I sleep to dream I wake,
blurring their grainy contours by mistake,
yet, being mortal, as I puff and pant,
am lashed by time to listen to his rant.
He purses up his lips. He snorts and spits,
recriminating, 'Nothing you do fits.
So, doubled self, self-doubter, rave and scream,
sleeping to dream you wake and waking dream.'

First kiss

Aroused awareness (body's being) dawns,
then, flaring, flushes tides along the blood.
Delightful, light-full, double touch that burns,
this kiss cuts lies away with fleshy blade.
All previous loss (hope, fear) loosens and drains
and our most potent self-deceits lie floored.
All argument, integument of brains,
all prejudices, wash away in flood.
Eureka moment. Past illusions fall.
'We love each other.' Now we realise
uncovering (discovering) is all.
Mists tumbling waft away from widened eyes,
humbled, mere human, doubly huge and small,
in wonder, under widened, deepening skies.

You

Possessing and possessed by *now*, in casting
a self (with no intent to mean to mean),
you, face here-now and outside, everlasting,
are you *now's* shadow, window, core or sheen?
You merest glimpse, glance, graze, you scent of scent,
my chaser, my outflanker, my outrider,
pitched on this point in your transhumant tent,
you-foreigner, you-stranger, you-outsider,
you double loss and gain in double bond
ever escaping elsewhere, out beyond
this *this*, this *now* and *here*, this *much* and *most*,
come join with me, come back, come yoke, commingle
your image, oscillating, double-single,
now with your other self, my other's ghost.

Identities

I am not double-barrelled

I am not double-barrelled. Family trees
are for sound sleepers who wake up alert.
I come from a long line of nobodies
who spat blood and just loved. That was their lot.
My folks' huge hopes for love could not be dashed
at lowdown stakes, or from the heights of gallows,
and when their mouths were split and jawbones smashed
they sealed lips and forgave most of the blows.
In love, they swallowed smiles, took hurried steps,
avoided high noons, honeymoons and homes,
quivering with fear even at shadows' shapes.
Inheriting tough, hunched up, crooked frames,
they misfired every arrow from hope's quiver
and all they aimed at floated off down river.

after the Serbian of Oskar Davičo

Anybody's guess

'Whoever *I* is isn't for the taking
by any *thou*, who knows it can't be done.
Such clutch or crutch would merely be heartbreaking
(merely?),' says anybody, not no-one,
'for boundaries deceive, their petty plots,
both *mine* and *thine*, incongruously blurred.
To tell such plural *ares* from these *are nots*
a knotted, knitted business, and absurd.'
Away! away! for *I* would fly with *thee*
adroitly through (beside) *our* blinkeredness.
Beside sweet living streams, *thou* tidest *me*
through *notness*, throughout everlastingness.
Seeing who sees who is, who will decline
such questings – whether *his, hers, yours* or *mine*?

19

Being aloof

Then who is *they*, or who *are*, and who *you*,
being so hidden in this present guise
that anyone in right mind might assign
a value or a definition to?
The speaker (being here?) seems vanished – through
(even behind?) these word-nets, line on line –
knit, meshed or trammelled in a paradise
well lost, if ever *I* and *thou* were true.
So, varnished, vanquished, vanished values, why
should we pretend you true or right or proof
of worth or honour, still less constancy,
knowing that right and wrong are warp and woof
of *we, you, they, he, she, it, thou* and *I* –
being pure fiction, someone else, aloof.

Pronouns

So pronouns, you're reversible. Who cares
then whether what you think we think you mean
by occupying us (quite unawares),
claiming control over what's heard, felt, seen,
and head, and heart – as if you were defined –
gets questioned, doubted, challenged? Rightly so.
You're keys to neither consciousness nor mind
or anything we think you think or know.
When *you* means *I, we, they* – or anyone,
what *self* or *ego* is remains beyond
the scope of any pronoun's lexicon
or grid, co-ordinate or reference bond.
You're nothing more than map-pins, local tags,
not wraps or skins but belts to girdle rags.

Hence into suchness

Hence into suchness – if such suchness be
available for purchase, loan, hire, theft.
Thrift calls, suspecting magnanimity
of reckless overbrimming, through a cleft
that opens on such panoramic vistas
self-loss, and even loss of self's desire,
record as flak through terminal transistors.
Blue dream? White noise? Mere background hum? Pale fire?
Not to be bought? Or known? Is there no rent
to tempt us to pay out the asking price
suchness demands be dissipated, spent
on entering where *now*'s non-paradise
(accreting *notness* as our instants live)
gets unmade, made, recursive-iterative?

Past and through

Punning, might I get thróugh words to the un-
knowable knots loosened beneath their reach,
past pasts' and futures' fastnesses, past speech,
past where no speech's echo could outrun
the beckonings of silence unbegun,
where not so much as pre-word, chirp or screech,
could send sign or bear meaning, each to each,
to particles fired out from some new sun?
Shielding the clarity that *being* shares
with *notness*, when time leaps in insight's flares –
notness being flint-spark and its afterglow –
I *no* and *yes* I *yes* and *no* I *no*,
as these words, spiralling fireflies, pump wings
and lift, unravelling these offerings.

Then doubts devour

Then doubts devour. How do (does) *I* exist,
savaged by knife-thrusts from *another*, who
attacks behind each figure I move through
till self is carved up, piecemeal? How resist
such lacerations? Or, failing that, insist
these *I*'s be gathered, stitched back, and stay true
to 'entity', 'identity' – *me* – *you*?
The Self, sequestered like a crag in mist,
glimpsed out of focus, seems quite out of range.
Blurry in outline, vague in shape and size,
it yields no definition, edge or border.
Familiar-foreign, intimate yet strange,
it baffles searching intellect and eyes,
resonating another (higher?) order.

I empty and I fill

A sponge that soaks up pasts (time left behind),
plus what now moves, plus much of what is still
vague, termless, virginal, in terms of *will*
(unimaged, undecided, undesigned)
may be what *I* is – should *I* be defined
by entity. I empty and refill
with mass and definition tight until
my oceanic end, when de-confined
whatever *I* was blends into a pure
expanse of *notness*, in which nothing's sure,
a speckless speck, which (if it might be claimed
to have had movement) could not be a wave –
though, if the latter, what space might be named
let alone saved, in dust or bone in grave?

A conception

Can this unrealising mind conceive
its own annihilation? Being man
or woman born of woman means I can
imagine my own absence, even grieve
among the very mourners I'll bereave,
remembering gone selves with kin and clan,
and each, oh what a skilled tragedian,
clutching and begging others not to leave.
But might this single death to others be
if not first person, singular to *me*?
Although, pure plural, death's forays and raids
will batter down this body's barricades,
mortality – dear – final – finitude –
I greet you now with stiffened fortitude.

Stone

What if the stone saw you? What if the stone
had eyes in every molecule, to spy
on you? And if it had mouth to cry
and taste, and ears to distinguish tone
would it engage, or leave you well alone –
this block uncarved, this craggy mystery –
or contemplate, admire you, and thereby
respect your being's difference from its own?
Could we then read each other, stone, anew
within each other's presence, each unique,
each conscious *hitherto* and *hereunto*?
By staring at us, stone, would you then wreak
such havoc by transfixing us, right through,
that we should lose even our power to speak?

On Synchronicity

When anxious waiting stops

When anxious *waiting* stops and *wants* diffuse
and neither presses hard for consequence
then new views open, and receptive cues
bathe in a kind of floodlit innocence.
Through bones and organs and their folds and layers
fording the body's semi-porous skin
the unexpected may come streaming in
on sudden flood, catching one unawares.
When you no longer look, it's then you see,
when you stop listening consciously, you hear
unnoticed pattern, innate harmony,
and plural demarcations disappear.
Through mists of dream and daydream's musing haze
the self itself attains clear-focused gaze.

When it arrives

You are not focused, not on anything
when it arrives. It strikes you unawares.
It can't be faked, and no conceit prepares
its rendering, a subtle *now*-surrendering.
It has no antecedents. As for heirs
its will is *here-now,* which redeems its shares
as it alerts you in a listening –
a corrugated wavelike glistening –
to your whole self and world, each coiled in each,
infinite depth in infinite outreach.
Your being, adrift in daydream or faint daze
of blurry perturbation, misted haze,
is opened as a luminescent glaze
arrays the world of *this this this* in praise.

The flows of time

Nor is it just that time has different speeds
or that its currents currently compose
one passing river, or that this proceeds
through past to future. It's that *time-now* flows
not in some simple horizontal plane
but dips and peaks, in spirals, wells, coils, spools,
returning and re-gathering again
in centripetal-centrifugal pools
from so many dimensions and directions
and in such varied patternings and modes,
bearing such differing lightnesses and loads,
incursions, repetitions and inflections,
that what this present holds and overspills
is all time, as it fills, empties, refills.

When things fit

To note disparities, things that don't fit,
and then discover that in fact they do,
reveals reality as composite –
as pattern, which a common thread runs through.
Event and mind, blurred, latent, localise,
inner and outer gather, graze, connect,
apparent counter-movements focalise
and suddenly, the human intellect
is borne on such a flood of energies
that, though you'll always fail to fathom how,
what once seemed unimaginable is
actualised in an all-inclusive *now*.
Delight inflects the heart. Welling surprise
opens your pores, streams through your hands and eyes.

Anomalous phenomena

'Anomalous phenomena', though strained
through test and retest, aren't attuned to give
hoped-for results. Rather, being engrained
fast in resistance, their prerogative
appears to be to baffle, block, occlude,
refuse to open intervening valves
and, nonchalantly, carelessly, exclude
the curious watcher from the things themselves.
But should the watcher once stop watching and
let focal points lie fallow till they blur,
then things, without support or helping hand,
may of their own accord begin to stir.
So could it be that things themselves have eyes
enabling *them* to take *us* by surprise?

Fuse

'Between apprehension's insistent instant
and this awareness of it, lies the germ
of split consciousness, irreducible torment
of being, as if intentionless intent
were trapped here too.' *But no.* In the blink term
that holds act and longing, egg admits sperm
in unique momentum. Form (be)gets content.
And as from topsoil the peristaltic worm
wriggles its way out, look, up there, a lark
soars on cloud-morning, singing. And as fact
la(n)ces world itself and being in stark
brilliant focus – so touching, touched, intact
world and *this* connect, fusing time and sky
with reverent irrelevant perceiving *I*.

Things constellate

Things constellate and cluster round the norm
and when they press hard in, the core explodes.
Form mirrors content, content mirrors form,
but when the mirror bursts, the tempered codes
that kept things' balances, their parity,
can hold themselves no longer, and instead
the rules that governed *this* reality
splinter in paradigms unheralded
by hope or expectation. Things change gear,
new types press out in forms unbroached before
and unencountered elements appear
from seething chaos, whose erupting core
thrusts *notness* through *here-now*. Beauty and fear
heal clean by fire or, clashing, knot in war.

Approach me not

The cavern where the dreamer sleeps enclosed
by panes of consciousness is made of stuff
permeable to eternity. Enough
of limitations grammars have imposed
on waves of seeing, traced on haze and seeming.
Approach me not. An *elseness* in me wakes
out through this body's gauze, its wefted walls,
so distance and horizons shed their skin
and *everything* and *nothing* tumble in
past ordering, past patterning, past scheming.
The bond, appearance, stretches taut and breaks
tensed contraries that differentiate
and *I*, whatever *I* was, cannot wait.
A burned moon rises, and a black sun falls.

After eternity : a dialogue

First there was void, and then a soundless bang.
Time is an arrow, not a boomerang.
Life is a knotted string that time pulls straight,
spun out by change and chance into your fate.
While swallows gather and the summer dies
love is blinked out like summer's butterflies.
Love will play on for ever, never trying,
never striving or dying, time defying.
After eternity we live out time.
The bell strikes but you cannot hear the chime.
We live to praise, to celebrate and treasure
infinite presences no clock can measure.
The lock is timeless and the hand is yours
to turn the key that opens all time's doors.

Time's porous skin

Time's true to things in ambiguities
which in their fragile fractal repetitions
seem torn, despite their continuities,
a stuttered morse, dependent on transitions.
Bridges and bonds of parataxis in
time's fine but incompletely woven forms
stretch full of holes, as if its porous skin
were pocked by many more dimensions' storms.
I lose them in my waking but in sleep
past time I track their sheens beneath the crust
this consciousness must haul across time's deep
unfathomable ocean, bearing trust
this trawling (trailing, trialling) will keep
signing me well until this *I* is dust.

Passage

Titanic

So flutter, twitch and bat your bloody brows
and, yes, remind us daily that you're waiting
adroit and subtle Death, ingratiating
your presence into all our *heres* and *nows*.
Our passage to you looms before the bows
beneath this wind's boom and beside the grating
drum of engines, under the understating
creakings of this vast hull where we carouse.
I won this passage on the only stake
mortality allowed. But you will never
peel from my heart a single kiss or sever
one second of shared consciousness or break
what love made from us for the other's sake
though afterwards we drown in you forever.

Give Time

So take your time, enjoy it at your leisure,
relish your hours, yet watch them pass away,
or save time, and relinquish every pleasure
in mourning for a morning or a day,
or, keep time, and tap out its subtle measure
dancing in rings until steps go astray –
but give time, and receive time's finest treasure,
fountains of stars, the frost-furred Milky Way.
Move through time's inner rooms and corridors
and die imprisoned behind granite walls,
trace each of time's results from its first cause
and hear time's muffled echoes and footfalls,
then listen to time clapping its applause
and beg for time for extra curtain calls.

Allegro

Does life exist *before* death? Well, if so
it can't be this one, stacked with suffering.
The blind land where the one-eyed man is king,
through which there spreads a curious warm glow,
has hair-cracks in it, gaps through which pulsate
plashed across spacetime, far suns' alien beams,
sounds never heard, faint perfumes beyond dreams,
waves that won't burn, although they penetrate.
Yet that's not it. A kind of *elseness* slips
through in rare inklings, managing to float
across and past the inner dark that grips
and limits us. And even though the pivot
balancing real and unreal scarcely tips
the bitter lump loosens that blocked the throat.

after the Greek of Nasos Vayenas

Then

Not now, but then? But when might *then* take place
or will or did or does, or could or would?
If *then* means subsequence or consequence,
something *about to*, whether bad or good,
leave off, *then*, playing both sides of the fence
of *here-and-now*, and kindly have the grace
despite self-loss and lack of likelihood
to free this present tense of your pretence.
To each event, *then*, you imply *before*,
a time-connected interface for action,
expectancy, anticipation, dread –
hence, what's owed, borrowed or inherited,
time's key to the unopenable door
of *next* – this finite present's liquefaction.

Me from the future

The opposite of *yet* is not *not yet*.
The antonym for *not yet* is *already*.
Is what is gotten bygone? I forget
but take this gradual waking slow and steady.
Each day I wake to plenty, and still more
(to *come*, to *be*, to *be-come*) swells and calls
me from the future marked *not yet,* in store,
plashing through fountains, streams and waterfalls.
Yet seems to have a question mark beside.
Before comes *not*. Doubt and surprise come after.
This dialectic, after you have died,
runs out like air and water, leaves and laughter.
Me from the future? Not yet quite awake?
Here do I hear the clasps of my time break?

This far, so soon

This far, so soon? Already Master Death
tugs at the leash invisibly he holds
around my throat and catches at the breath
this flesh enfolds, that through this flesh unfolds.
Because my Master needs me, like a clown
I bring him twigs and bones and wag my tail
and, panting, hunt to bring his quarry down
and close and sniff him out, until lungs fail.
Yapping or growling out my little song,
so help me, canine Gods, I swear I will
serve, entertain him, all my dog's life long,
even though *he*'s the prey I bay to kill.
Like any slave I know my Master's mind
so lead him onward, merciless, dumb, blind.

An ephemeral mark

An ephemeral mark, not even a stain,
a dampness you thought might dry after rain,
sprinkled or dappled, unfolded or stretched,
worn for a moment but not even sketched
let alone engrained in the core of things,
the opening bars of the score s/he sings
or rather hums, so low it seems no more
than leaves rustling on the derelict floor
of a roofless abandoned house, whose door
stutters on rusted hinges as it swings –
noting blank daze swamp meaning, hum flood speech,
s/he swabs you down with anechoic screech
whose graze ekes out your final sucked-in gasp,
your rattling anti-whisper, last-ebbed rasp.

Fall on my heels

Fall on my heels and trip me as you please
my fellow traveller Time, I shall still grope
my way along the road, though on my knees,
deprived of limbs and eyes, but not of hope.
Dog all my days with sorrow till my end,
ravage my cheeks with furrows, steal my powers
of movement, insight, love, take every friend
and empty the veined vessels of my hours.
Though stripped and crippled, wizened and half mad,
without the will to ask or strength to take
or memory to dream of all I've had,
I'll go, Time – when you face me – wide awake,
not begging you to stand awhile at bay
but smiling as you suck my breath away.

Blackout, hospital

The nothingness that lurks between heartbeats
opened. Four times I tumbled through a pause
(gap, gulf, hiatus, void), to where the laws
of time collapse in serial defeats.
Time bent and folded, creased in coils and pleats
between *will be* and *was*, effect and cause.
Yet somehow I've escaped Death's ready jaws
to lie here, stunned, between these cool white sheets.
The ward is quiet. Only I'm awake
bathed in chilled sweat, head swimming. But I'm back.
No pain or fear, no danger, no heartbreak.
I am alive. I'll get back on the track.
So, nothingness, you'll have to wait a bit
before you fetch me down into your pit.

I dreamed I slept

I dreamed I slept, and in that sleep I dreamed
and from that double dream interior woke
and walked in a closed courtyard. Someone spoke
behind me, and I turned. A dark girl beamed
a smile at me and said, 'Just as you seemed
in dream to dream, so by the double stroke
of waking into waking, from this yoke
you've mutely shouldered, may you be redeemed.'
So when I enter my last mortal sleep
after dreams end and I vacate this shell
will I then wake and, doubly waking, keep
some mirror of that courtyard in my skull
and, back inside it, rising from the deep
notness of death, sleepwalk, or wake instead?

A Discipline

A discipline

I need this discipline to frame my stand
against my death. Too weak indeed, seeing He
eventually cannot but topple me
hardly winking or batting brow or hand.
I, like a tower of balanced feathers, fanned
by merest sneeze or cough, or rather puff
of anti-breath, will cave in quick enough
as Death deems fit and Doom and Fate have planned.
Against *my* death? No, against all! I cry.
Yours and yours, friends, comrades! Too weak indeed
to hold such feathered Babels? Well then, fly
little art, and though we'll all fall, all bleed,
gather up human suffering and need
and on *these* wings sweep Death out of the sky.

Death moves towards my death

Death moves *towards* my death. He faces me
all-knowing, but prefers to hide and wait
in mist and cloud so that I cannot see
when, where or how I shall disintegrate.
Death moves *behind* my death. I go ahead
at least while I have mind and consciousness.
Whether I dance or feel my feet like lead
I must move forward. There is no redress.
Death moves *before* my death, anticipating
trivial details – time, place, weather, wind.
Together, in a dance of double waiting
we move, each other's double, as if twinned.
Whether he moves *towards, behind, before,*
I stand here present, prescient, at Death's door.

I work, but nothing I do works

I work, but nothing I do works. I toil
but still have nothing whole or good to show.
My trials all (before completion) spoil.
Craft, yes, I have. But lack ingathered flow.
And yes, I possess 'talent'. But the will?
Do I have that? Strong-backboned ruggedness?
Blind courage necessary to fulfil
ambition? And determined doggedness?
I'm sworn to competition only with
my self. No other can defeat me. But
that ever-present looming monolith
(before whose face I cannot dare to strut)
past self-eroding scratchmarks won't impart
the faintest hint of path on map or chart.

I longed for fame

I longed for fame. It would not be bestowed
nor will – till dead – if then – of that I'm sure.
But I'll walk on unswerving though obscure
as any traveller on the shimmering road
burning to ash behind us. Hopes that glowed
like lamps before me hereby I abjure
and all the lovely outlines whose allure
by ways and waysides jarred me where they flowed.
Away sweet jangling images! You blurred
the coiled lines of the way I had no choice
but track and follow to the brimming rim
of *now*, in flood. Listen – a dull brown bird
is pouring song out on spontaneous voice
across the sky. What impulses fire him?

It goes with me hard

It goes with me hard
when the work's marred
by my own folly
whether from desire,
hope, melancholy
or by passion's fire.
Being too coarse and thick
to catch the quick
instantaneous flame
in substance not name,
I strike but fail to enter
marrow – core – centre.
Carve of me a reed
or mustard seed.

My stoic motive falters

My stoic motive falters. I've grown weak.
My longing to be loved, to be admired,
ranks higher with me than to be inspired.
Each time I parrot clichés as I speak
I want not to be true, but called *unique*
for phrases I have fashionably acquired
and so be held desirable, desired
by those I least respect. What fraud or freak
stuffed brimful with obtuseness and inanity,
crass vacancy, ingratiating vanity
could less inspire (excite, interest, amuse)
than I, in substituting *tastes* and *views*,
wit and *cuteness*, for truth? Time to cut down,
pompous old fool, false self-regarding clown.

Space, time, hope, work

My space – a nought,
a ringed zero caught
before or after thought.
My time – a meshed net
criss-crossed by loss and threat,
stretched between *then* and *yet*.
My hope – a taut string
wound by suffering
around thing and thing.
My work – for a word
unimaged, unheard,
behind the mind's absurd
strings, wires and cages
that curb passion's rages.

Come, word-rows

Come, word-rows, solid sturdy measured planks,
sawn, planed and jointed carefully – here, take
these densely loaded meanings, and don't break
but stand by one another, guarding flanks.
Sawn shelves, hold safe these phrases, lined in ranks,
built not to fall (split, cave, creak, crack or shake)
but to survive tsunami and earthquake.
Sure, stable lines, you'll serve, and earn my thanks.
Yet, grainy, knotted trunks, being so dense
will you support what inescapably
must burst through rigid syllables and thence
wing leaf-like on wind-currents and sail free?
How will you brace to touch, graze, skim or sense
what strains and stresses for transparency?

Into these poems

Into these poems go
my full body and mind
and soul and spirit also –
no part gets left behind.
Anything smaller or less
would be meaningless.
But then doubt creeps in –
I haven't given my all
for I hold fear within –
of the poem's call.
I'll give my last breath
this side death
and for this to break through
death, I'll give you too.

Will

Not just this flesh is mortal, but this *will*
will also perish from the works I pass
down out through time: steel blades, stilled blades of grass,
my hieroglyph and cuneiform. No skill
I had, possessing me through time, shall fill
these works' defects with compensating force.
Therefore let *will* take its predestined course
and serve as scaffold for the final kill.
So, then will *will* droop, falter, wither, fall
and disappear (the common miracle)?
Or will a strength, resilient, apart
from *will* (will's soul?) live on, here, in this art –
so these works stand, unexplicated, clear,
crystal, and independent of me here?

Notness

Notness

The passages of time being relative
and its dimensions being infinite
now filters all time through the finest sieve
in morsels so minute they'd scarcely fit
even this bowl of light in which we live –
if time were not repatterned, bit by bit,
instant on instant, through the requisite
paths our destinies make here (break, take, give).
Though time's flecked passing be a passing torment
watching pasts go (irrevocable rift)
in this most rich, most full, excessive moment
(already gone) resides the finest gift,
the *notness* in the presence of the torrent
and each dust flake translucent that I sift.

Notness, in doubt

In doubt I started between truth and error
bred in my being by experiment.
I ended here behind a gate of terror
my ego opened for me. In I went.
I passed by here in dark. Hyperbole
attracted me, through which I made a maze.
Oh, such connections and disjunctions I
found here prismatic in refracting rays.
Frictions and fractions fascinated me,
levels of nothings and their underlayers
criss-crossed, unnoticed, comprehensively –
from which I dug forgotten praise and prayers.
At edges and frontiers where I debated
meaning and notness interpenetrated.

Notness, mirroring

I is and are. *Amness* itself's a land
hemmed in by oceanic death and strange
(as infinitely distant, out of range)
as that far shore, imagined but unscanned,
where on both sides of *entity* you stand
but never manage ever to arrange
within the scoping of perpetual change
what terms and endings you'd spied out or planned.
For as you turn, returning, all your *I*'s
are hung in facing mirrors, fast retreating,
fast shrinking back, identically repeating
into a *notness* where exhausted eyes
film over, glazing, in a self-defeating
infernal groping for lost paradise.

Notness, end

A wintry light, a hinterland of snows
whose silver dawns are garlanded in ice,
a planet decked in diamond repose,
a gleaming pearl, a crystal paradise.
Notness shall greet this morning, turn its face
towards its pale sun, hovering, as if lost.
Notness will hang in luminescent grace
among these ghosts of *when,* in flowers of frost.
A tapestry of nothing, static, blends
bland, faded, in this knot that *notness* is.
This is where *when* itself watches tail-ends
of things implode in singularities.
Once here trees grew, birds sang, and rivers coursed.
Now *notness* falls. Their final holocaust.

Notness, unapparent

Irradiated with a billionfold
more possibilities than actualised
(imagined, thought, dreamed, pictured, half-surmised),
even as you arrive, untouched, untold,
you fade, dissolve, as if into the hold
of what cannot be held, or crystallised,
or recognised, even hypothesised,
and still less patterned into any mould.
A conjuror's cloth, now you collapse in pleats
of unapparent *notness*, where before
you'd seemed to flash, curl, wave in banners, sheets
of lightning storms and rainbows by the score.
You were a plethora, a feast of treats,
that now are nothing, skinless, without core.

Bogomil

Whether a hinted half-traced face appears
sudden in dark or light from the last wave
of grief that beat and carved onto this grave
some message that might mock oncoming years,
like *Rest In Peace,* in spite of mourners' tears,
or whether doubt, dread, terror made them rave
because from nothing they might nothing save
of sweet life and its sultry atmospheres –
if you could scry that face, might you then give
meanings back to lost symbols spelt upon
summers in Sumer or in Babylon –
and so, by tracing serifs, sift or sieve
in nets of light, worlds still to come, or gone,
or catch them through dark glass, in negative?

Aye and Nay

Things move away from one another, all
in all directions, yet the life that grew
into this fulness *now* contracts into
a spot, knot, dot, oh far less than a small
dust speck, point, infinitesimal ball,
and all the joys, friends, pleasurings I knew
and laughters, games and glories we moved through
follow the wheel-rule: fall-rise, rise-and-fall.
Therefore I *aye* the *yes* and *know* the *no*.
Growing through each, I glory in their flow
and, not to be entangled in the mess
wanting would make by want of stillness, or
willing things followed plans I'd scanned before,
I also *aye* the *nay* and *know* the *yes*.

Yes and No

I *yes* the things I *no*. I *no* the *yes*.
I can't help it. I *no* and *yes* them both.
I crave the infinite but finiteness
folds and sustains me in its patchwork cloth.
Wrapped in its wings, strings, things, under duress
though I would work my way out like a moth
I knot and unknot spacetime, and address
myself to things' contractions, patterns, growth –
how the entire known universe *expands*,
still holding *me* enfolded in its weft.
May I hold this in mind too, in these hands,
when *yes* deserts and *no* leaves me bereft.
I *yes* the *no* in *no's* and *yes's* core
shimmering between after and before.

Statues

in the temple of Eros and Thanatos

Immortal volunteers and candidates,
they chime long echoes in our consciousness.
Here, two are locked. They kiss, embrace, caress.
He kneels, she squats. Another watches, waits.
Two more in passion's combat-stress rehearse
pressures of flesh and muscle against skin.
Naked, another hurls a javelin
while two in tunics casually converse.
There, warriors in ranks ensure a king
shall make safe passage to the other shore.
In clay, wood, marble, metal, all abhor
movement, which they have passed, and suffering.
These words though, carved like them, call out and breathe.
Life leaps here through them as they writhe and seethe.

Notness, puckering

This *notness,* puckering the skin of *now,*
grazing the moment moving and at rest,
unfolds (combs out, outspreads) the very best
that I could ever know, guess or avow.
We cannot grasp it, neither *I* nor *thou*
shivering, separate. Yet how we're bless'd
since here eternity's distilled, compressed
in random oneness every *where*-and-*how.*
Being both point with no end or dimension
and finite mark that cuts and knots the reign
of what's gone, by the future's intervention,
tumbling through gravity and surface tension
now pools here like a lake from threads of rain,
full drops felled, falling down a window pane.

Now

Now

Now holds all that's perceivable to sense
and more-than-senses (meditation? prayers?)
in concentration, pure, refined, intense.
Now abstracts (from potential) abstract layers
to concretize them in self-evidence,
for instance, in what happens to the hairs
on arms, and skin-pores, when coincidence
shivers the frame and radiant fulness flares,
or when a sound sparks off a resonance,
thrilling and chilling, from the gentlest airs.
Now's curious landscape (flat, steep, deep, thin, dense)
subsumes all borders and contains all *wheres*
in innocence and in obedience,
contraries coexisting unawares.

Now, point

How I am flooded by the giant size
of this one point, this *now*, this hollow drum
of momenthood, whose mode and medium
consist of glory, radiance, surprise
(phantom, come, gone) before I realise
this mini-heaven, aspiration's sum
rounded in fulness, emptiest vacuum,
cannot be held (distilled) as paradise.
And though this point of *now* (this full cup) holds
nothing but *notness* without skin or core
being infinitesimal *and* one
see how its quick transparency unfolds
pluralities of things just as they are
flickering past no sooner than begun.

Now, crumbling

Now, crumbling in the vast imperative
of arrowed curves and carvings, falls like rain,
a plaintive, pliant interrogative
pouring away. Nor will *you* come again.
No presence could sustain, less still summate
the timescapes strewn across your roundedness.
Were you a verb, how would you conjugate
to ramify (breach, clasp) unboundedness?
Still, you move ever constant in your weight
of weightless nothing. Like a steady river
you are what's *given*, gift that gives your giver
this this, immediate, importunate,
on the specific onrush of your flow
whether we shall accept your gift or no.

Now, brimming

Now, brimming, spilling surplus, calls *more more*
to every drop and morsel of the real.
Though full in plenty, presence cannot heal
this *now* of incompleteness or restore
eternity through time or evermore
envelop this one moment with a seal
to stamp it still and separate, or reveal
more than it is. Its surface *is* its core.
Now, never static, will not isolate
itself from the continuum of space-time
through synaesthetic sense, or more sublime
transcendence of itself, or doom or fate.
Now fades and falls away like any quantum
leaving no trace, ghost-speck or shadow-phantom.

Now, drum

Now, hollow drum, old knot, new pleated fold,
mere point, fine spectrum, radiating waves
through time's continuum – thrumming loom that weaves
new fabrics on this energetic field
matted through matter, uncoiled and unfurled
across the dust-swept patterns of our lives –
no sooner swells and breaks than ebbs and leaves,
self-emptying each instant it has filled.
Is this then nothing but the drum the dream
of being patters out its morse upon?
Since *now* repeats with neither gap nor seam
between (within) each wave, its antiphon,
eliding all *now*s on a curved light beam,
how then can *now* be ousted or outshone?

Now, cup

To the Shekhinah, again

Spillage through *now* of vast eternities
won't be contained. *Now* floods and overbrims
coursing through organs, spreading out to limbs
joy (energy) to all extremities.
Perfection, borne on time, disperses currents
into *now*'s hollow chalice (bowl, pool, lake,
vessel, strong-standing, that won't crack or break)
to overflow in tricklings, cascades, torrents.
And so this cup runs over. Yes, it's true
excess of plenty quickens eyes that you
keep turning to me through refracted rays
sprayed under waterfalls by rainbow haze.
Now, transverse to time's flows, re-empties, fills
as, poured and pouring, glory overspills.

A point, a cup, a drum

A point, a cup, a drum, a gate that swings
back and forth, tempting, and then clangs shut, fast,
a meeting glance, a feather fluttering past,
a vista in a vista, packed with *things*
and each, when gone, rampant with echoings
of *next* and *afternext*, bred from the *last*,
ghosts of a needle's eye glimpsed through *now*'s vast
arena, spreading through concentric rings,
and though no *now* may ever come again
this *now*, its *then-past* and *then-next* stay wound,
unbroken, in a double spiral chain
of pastness and futurity around
one single coil of presence, to entrain
now in its knot of *notness* stretched and bound.

Concerning music

Seeing that through this *now* flow fine and firm
currents of time, directed in more ways
than eyes perceive or intellect can term
even though portioned through divided days,
and hearing in this *now* pure *notness* drum
its echoing note (eternity revealed?)
unclouded, light-filled, against background hum
of *what-is* and *would-be*, together sealed –
may I in ways I've never dared before
smile, and express this smiling through me spread
as presence, not mere resonance or mime
and though swept by alternate hope and fear,
haunted by ghosts both unborn and long dead,
find in this *now* my proper space in time?

Here is no mourning

Here is no mourning for what has not been.
These sounds of wind and rain on drums and strings
the elements themselves play through the seen
world we live in, on clustered, cluttered things,
prints of the rainbow, woodsmoke's whorls and scents,
snails' shells, rams' horns, hissing sands on dunes –
in hardy harmonies or wavering tunes
all echo, *are* each others' instruments.
Scant, scattered, thronged or banked in murmurings,
things being what they are, what they might mean
gets sounded, filled, on resonance between
waves' mountings, curves, arrivals, vanishings.
Such subtle blending of this *now*'s refrain
coils *now* in *always*, now, and now again...

To light, in an interior

What else but you supports the strings and veils
meshed into things' appearances and cores?
Sifter of shadows each thing underscores
(*thinghood* itself being what your grace entails)?
What else but you is pivot for the scales
weighing this mazing criss-crossing white gauze
of net curtains against our walls and floors
shimmering or darkened, as day mounts and fails?
Fulcrum of diamond, balancing between
each thing and thing, space each thing must evince,
we cannot track you, but infer you, since
you are the means by which all things are seen
pouring *now*, overbrimming, into *this*,
measuring *this this* on your weightlessness.

Twiceness

Twiceness

Things' *twiceness* weighs and weights me, keeps me back,
too dense to float or fly off through the mind
and loose or lose myself there: double bind
inflicted on me by things' bric-à-brac
as if by arrows tumbling in attack
surrounding me. I stay *here* hemmed, confined,
cribbed, pinioned, intermeshed, trapped, intertwined
in matter's knots, stretched trim, taut, without slack.
And yet, thin things, although you grasp me here,
however tight you hold me tangled, bound
in depth, seam, surface, layer or veneer,
by curving and reflecting light and sound
it's by your ways, waves, rhythms that I steer
flights into glory from this echoing ground.

Once, twice…

Considering this onceness, its uniqueness,
I think it as eternity condensed
into one point, unscathed, uninfluenced
by any *else*, having no hole or weakness.
Hence *now* is what holds nothing (being *isness*
itself) in pure perfection, made, unmade
only to bloom, not bud, grow, wither, fade
and with no other state, shape, role or business.
Yet *now* repeats, repeats, and every one
of all its furled or pleated nothingnesses
(out of last *notness*, whether dreamed or done)
melts, merges, in the next *now* it addresses.
If now's unique, twiceness, its forfeiture
yields it to *after* through and from *before*.

The doubling

The doubling of a thing into a sign
and back again along the two-way strings
perception and phenomena entwine
constitutes thinghood. Each thing, rippling rings
outward through spacetime, gets remade, refurled
(recurled, returned, retwirled) on circumstance
to *in*form, *re*form *this*. And so this world
whirls, whorls things in proliferating dance.
Things' thinghoods replicate complexities
whose fractal echoes mime the miracle
this *here-now* is – recurring geometries
of bounty (fulness, plenty, overspill),
excessive, but just so, in all that is –
a Star of David in a daffodil.

David

You stand, oblivious of praise or pride
before the pebble in your sling is thrown,
one moment in a man solidified,
roused by your sculptor from rejected stone,
flesh frozen as in godhood, limpid marble,
limbs patterned after Adam Kadmon's mould,
hushed presence of both Iliad and Bible,
championing freedom, unique, manifold.
Time slices lives, but you restore it, whole.
In this your moment *after* and *before*
close ranks and settle, as if history's goal
(past dialectics, oppositions, war)
were gathered in a single body-soul
whose long patience will outlast *evermore*.

Reasons, cores, sheens

What reasons I have come into this world
for stay mysterious. Far too soon I leave.
The spaces, signs, materials that I love,
domesticate and harvest here, by willed
deliberate endeavour, will run wild
behind my buried back, and if they live
at all beyond me, do so as mere slave
to waves that welled in them, then ebbed and swirled.
Mostly we scarcely graze or scratch the skin
things in their scattering glories here surround
and flood us with. Whoever enters in
soon finds there is no core to sky or ground,
only more pleatings, interleaved so tight
their filmy sheens seem solid in this light.

Dot

Illuminated by concentric rings
pulsating their own radiance, this dot
of consciousness, this point that sobs and sings
is governed by what is. There's not a jot
this universe consists of – quanta, strings –
apparent among images that things
cast into moving patterns – that is not
keyed to this context (fabric, mesh, maze, plot)
of undulations, spirals, mirrorings.
Without co-ordinates of space and time
and, who knows, many more dimensions still,
each repetition, variation, chime
that makes this *now* our common miracle
would bear scant pressure, weight, flow, stress or rhyme
or let this empty purse of *notness* fill.

Text and intertext

This moment is perfected paradise.
Its sudden flare could not be more complete.
Then comes the next and grips it like a vice
stamping it out at each new moment's feet.
Each crushes being opened. None will last,
no sooner aired, dispersed in airiness.
Not that each moment betters each one past,
disgorged, exhausted, spent in weariness,
or that each one's not infinitely vast.
To each its *thisness here*, its veryness.
And so it goes, next, next, and afternext,
each cracking each no sooner than begun.
As *Midrashim* illuminate a text
each heaven breaks and rémakes each last one.

A resonance

My other came. His glance did not offend.
He stood between this building and a ground
that faded into mist at its far end.
No bird in branches made a single sound.
'This is my other and my brother,' said
a voice born out of nowhere in my head,
'but which one breathes on this side, and which dead,
is quite uncertain here, despite the dread
that occupies you each in double presence.'
This happened in (across) two sets of eyes
through quiet, in a kind of reticence.
The hills said nothing in their paradise
but echoed, chiming, in a resonance
as fast as light, past shock, past (passed) surprise.

Ground

This ground itself is perfect. It supports
the weight this body loads on it, plus all
they, you and *I* may muster, ferry, toll
across these worn or undiscovered routes.
It's doubly real. It bears and buries thoughts
and echoes and reflects them when they call.
Answering body with response of soul,
it gives, takes evidence, and proves, refutes.
A gift fore-granted, wonder-filled, felt, free,
this solid ground is made of constancy,
for though our passage here is briefer far
than those of tortoise or sequoia tree,
it bears us up. It holds up what we are.
It stands for what we know, have been, shall be.

Walking

On ground that holds me, steadying my feet,
I walk this world and breathe. The ready air
flows, follows, billows round me everywhere,
assuring, reassuringly complete.
Though infinitely varied, things repeat
in rhythms, waves, expansions that they share
with all else that's unique, beyond compare.
Each flaw or stain in glass, each grain of wheat,
each mole or wrinkle, every seam or pleat
in nature's fabric, every pore or hair
bears its own features, futures, stress, print, *flare*.
Miraculous, reverberating world,
filled with new things unfurling and unfurled
as I walk down this ordinary street…

For an Unborn Child

My life is the horizon

My life is the horizon of this page
these words go down beneath (your eyes) and kill me,
for leaving me in silence here, they will me
a death of sorts, that this may come of age
and what sets here, set so that it may rise
where you lie still asleep, and strew a dawn
over (that sea) your mind, you not yet born,
plashing pale light through first-time-opened eyes –
meaning, you give me life, you still unbreath,
still unmade, unimagined, unconceived
and still unmargined in a human doom.
Though with each word I breathe I draw a death,
you raise a second Lazarus from the tomb
these words have drawn around me while I grieved.

These subtle seasons

These subtle seasons' easy to-and-froing
wipe us away like insects from a pane
and carelessly ensure that, after going,
no single individual live again.
Sickle and scythe-blade, quickening or slowing,
cut close and fine, with or against the grain,
and though breed, type and tribe survive, keep going,
by breaking links, life strengthens its long chain.
So from its binding every life gets torn;
to make the book complete, each page is ripped.
But poetry, wraithlike, floating from the crypt
I hid this message in before Death stripped
these passing seasons from me, one fine dawn
Messiah-like in you, shall be reborn.

Since I unhesitatingly maintain

Since I unhesitatingly maintain
that I'll have no-one doubt or question I'm
wholly to blame for claiming you sublime –
like fingerprints whose spiral tracks remain,
in each gene here I've so pressed home my stain
as evidence and binding proof of crime,
so signed, stamped, sealed my guilt on future time,
imprinted it so deep, and pressed again
that, wanting to protect you from time's wrong
by making you immortal, nothing less,
have framed you here into a womb of song
and sealed in you your mother's loveliness.
You, child as yet unborn, would you forgive
this crime of mine, which makes you free to live?

With what bravado

With what bravado do I face the absurd
conclusion I must die, and consciousness
(this wonder) sink, and merge in fathomless
nothing, devoid of sound, speech, song or word –
as if time were annulled and backwards spurred
to pitch all *this* to zero. I confess
myself too bound in light's curved wovenness
to wish to quit it, burning or interred.
So is this world's appearance merely sham?
I'd wish not, but can't know, yet wish I knew.
I say *I'm not afraid*, but see I am.
You, vista I shall never set my eyes on,
child unconceived, blank page, mist-blurred horizon,
the *I*'s in this lie vacant for you too.

Nothing can never *No* you

Nothing can never *No* you with unknowing
nor bland oblivion graze you with its chill,
nor promises that freeze while falsely glowing
feign innocence, but know full well they'll kill.
No-one can never *No* you by ignoring
each single one of your uniquenesses,
nor shall malicious gossips, by point-scoring,
trace evidence of faults or weaknesses.
Nowhere can never *No* you by intent
nor gnaw you because malice made it fretful,
nor claim your passing over was not meant
because some fool or idiot was forgetful.
No time can never *No* you since this blesses
all traces, glimpses, signs of you with *Yeses*.

A Gift

A gift

You other, fellow, person, human, neighbour
whose kin cannot be proved, who yet are kin
though strange, and stranger far for being within –
you, sharer and divider of this labour
I toil at here (what for, who for? for you?
my therapy? my vanity, my pride?)
what will you make of this once I have died
and you look at or in, yet can't gaze through?
Our rendezvous (unmeasurable place)
is here, among, in, through, beneath, behind
these pages' words, and in their plural space,
for here we greet and touch, as kin, as kind.
So, singular distant friend, although your face
is strange, may we meet here in heart and mind.

Leash, long, flexed, wound, plaited

Leash, long, flexed, wound, plaited – how I have strained
at your presence, your pressured pull, limited scope,
hempen texture, stress of uncoiled, unfurled rope
stretched to your full, your end. Time, too, at mý end
shall be so tight, so taut, even now I reach, pained,
bonded, brimmed, bound by hope against all hope
of what cannot be done: to cut away, to grope
hillward, peakward, homeward, and despite my ills, mend.
Whatever I was dithers, withers, slithers, must be gone,
having learned, if anything, nothing more than this:
there's an unsutured rift running right through things
that senses can't grasp or gather or soul feed on
nor any *I* or *you* ever reach, touch or kiss,
so shall loss be better than best when *notness* rings?

The ghost of the nineteenth century

I've rescued you (and here you are again)
out of your trash bin, dumped in the waste land.
Yes, you can talk and walk here. As for pain,
you'll limp a bit a while. Here, take my hand.
Beauty – you were banished when the Big Guys
declared their war on everything 'effete'.
Again you rise: pink hum, blue buzz, white noise,
dawn-haze, glimpsed in glory over Mean Street.
They'd washed you out, then flushed you down a hole.
Naked or clothed, you'd been discredited.
Matter was what they wanted. Meat, not soul.
They'd thought you gone. You'd shrunk, paled, burned, scarred, bled.
Welcome back. It's time (*adagio*) to sing.
You've not changed much. And still you're ravishing.

I dreamed I wrote

I dreamed I wrote. A poem, long, assured,
impassioned, and composed in a white heat,
poured out of me. I set it down, complete,
perfected. And breathed, as if cleared, cleaned, cured
of every ill and anguish I'd endured
in making it. Surely my work would meet
acclaim, fame, recognition on the street…
I woke. My edifice collapsed, obscured.
I wrote *I dreamed*. And now, though breathless, dead,
through you who read this, I wake once again
imperfect, hopeful, agonised, as then.
I can't give you that poem, so instead
of what I'd rendered perfect in my sleep
I offer you this hint, this glint, to keep.

This book

His gates being open everywhere, and so
transparent no one notices they're there,
when my time comes, who knows how I shall go?
But whether I go senseless or aware,
this book, that has my name on it, is yours.
Once it was my gift. As my gift to you,
now I pass through the airless one-way doors
Death marks yet makes invisible to view –
leaving, I leave this book, my testament
to you, my unknown yet my close, dear friend,
its rightful bearer and recipient.
Since my identities have reached their end,
whoever you are or may or want to be,
the book is yours and I its history.

Afterword

This sequence of one hundred sonnets was composed between 1967 and 2013. The title, *Notness*, is an anagram of the word 'Sonnets'. The word 'Metaphysical' in the subtitle is, I hope, a pointer to some of the tendencies and intentions in and surrounding the title. The only further key – or, rather, hint – that I think needs to be offered here is that the so-called 'core' of *isness* is *notness*, just as at that of *notness* is *isnesss*: a never-ending dance. Others more adept at quieting the buzzing mind will know a good deal more about this than I do.

RB
CAMBRIDGE
JUNE 2014

Acknowledgements

Thanks to the editors who have published the following poems, sometimes in slightly different versions: 'I am not double-barrelled' by Oskar Davičo, *North Dakota Quarterly*, 61/1, Winter 1993; 'Give Time' and 'After Eternity', *Against Perfection*, Norwich: King of Hearts, 1999; 'Passage' and 'My stoic motive falters', *The London Magazine*, February 2003, and 'I longed for fame' and 'Bogomil', December 2003; 'True to your absence, glory', 'My motive falters' and 'Me from the future', *Society Today*, 5/6, May 2009; 'True to your absence, glory', *The Blue Butterfly*, Exeter: Shearsman Books, 2011; 'Bogomil' and 'I dreamed I slept', *Under Balkan Light*, Exeter: Shearsman Books, 2011; 'Allegro', *The Perfect Order* by Nasos Vayenas, eds. RB and Paschalis Nikoloau, London: Anvil Press Poetry, 2011; 'When anxious waiting stops', 'The flows of time', 'When things fit' and 'Things constellate', *Oxford Magazine* 33, 2012; 'Night bathing, Aegean', *Black Light / Luz negra*, bilingual edition, trs. Miguel Teruel and Paul Scott Derrick, Valéncia: JPM ediciones, 2012; 'Deep in that heart' and 'The Gulf' by Tin Ujević, *Twelve Poems*, trs. RB and Daša Marić, Bristol: Shearsman Books, 2013; 'Moon over sea', 'Siesta', 'Approach me not', 'Anomalous phenomena', 'Hence into suchness' and 'Insomniac presence', *broadsheet: new new zealand poetry* 11, Wellington: The Night Press, 2013; 'Statues', 'Walking', 'I dreamed I wrote' and 'Now, drum', *The Bow-Wow Shop*, February 2014; 'Stone', *Jewish Quarterly* 61:1, Spring 2014; 'When anxious waiting stops', *Caduceus* 88, 2014; 'This Scintillating Night', 'First Kiss' and 'Siesta', *Spokes* 10, 2014; 'It goes with me hard', 'Space, time, hope, work' and 'Into these poems', *Newsletter, Downing College Alumni Association*, 2014; 'David', *European Judaism* 47/2, Autumn 2014; 'It goes with me hard', 'Space, time, hope, work', 'Into these poems' and 'Radiance, palpable', *Oxford Magazine* 351, 2014; 'Now', *Long Poem Magazine* 12, 2014; 'DWELLING – FOR THE SHEKHINAH', *International Literary Quarterly* 22, 2015; 'The Doubling', 'Home', 'Once, twice…', 'A Resonance', 'Text and Intertext' and 'Dot', *Scintilla* 18, 2015; 'Blackout, hospital', 'Death moves towards my death', 'Ground' and 'Walking', *Oxford Magazine*, 2015; and 'When it arrives', 'Approach me not' and 'Now, cup', *Psychological Perspectives*, 2015.

My warmest thanks to Paul Scott Derrick, Kim Landers, Anne Stevenson and Henry Weinfield for their valuable critical comments on near-final drafts of this book; to Lee Moden for our discussions on time and the 'now'; to Catherine Pickstock for her illuminating writings, which have given me insights and directions, and in particular for generously allowing me to read her book *Repetition and Identity* in typescript, in March 2013, before its publication by Oxford University Press; to Roderick Main, for our ongoing correspondence on synchronicity and for his *Revelations of Chance: Synchronicity as Spiritual Experience* (State University of New York Press, Albany, 2007); to Robin Kirkpatrick, for our conversations; and to Paul Dominiak, for preparing a privately circulated edition of twenty-five of these poems for their first reading at Trinity College, Cambridge, in May 2013. I should also like to record my very special gratitude to Carl Schmidt, who in working closely and patiently with me on this book's final drafts not only offered astute critical comments and often transformative suggestions, but encouraged in me a heightened attentiveness to nuances of meanings, register, tone and musicality. Finally, I thank my wife Melanie Rein for her constant companionship and inspiration, as well as her invaluable comments through many stages of composition.

RB
CAMBRIDGE
JUNE 2014

References, Notes, Dedications

EPIGRAPHS

> Sources of epigraphs to this book are: Gershom Scholem, *On the Mystical Shape of the Godhead*, tr. Jochim Neugroschel, Schocken Books, New York, p. 173; Søren Kierkegaard, *Philosophical Crumbs*, tr. M. G. Piety, Oxford University Press, New York, 2009, p. 95; G. W. Leibniz, 'Letter to Rémont de Montfort', quoted by George R. Montgomery, 'Introduction', *Discourse on Metaphysics and The Monadology*, Dover Books, Mineola, 2005, xiv; Stephen Hawking, lecture at the Amsterdam Symposium on 'Gravity, Black Holes, and Strings', June 2, 1997, quoted in Brian Greene, *The Elegant Universe*, Vintage Books, London, 2000, p. 343; Catherine Pickstock, 'The Musical Imperative', *Angelaki, journal of the theoretical humanities*, 3/1, 1998, p. 24; and Paul Celan, 'The Meridian', *Collected Prose*, tr. Rosemarie Waldrop, Carcanet Press, Manchester, 2003, p. 52. The *Sefer HaBahir*, quoted by Gersholm Scholem in the first epigraph, is an early Kabbalistic text.

DWELLING – FOR THE *SHEKHINAH*, pp. 1–7

> To honour and remember Gershom Scholem (1897–1982).
>
> 'Dwelling' is associated with the *Shekhinah* (Hebrew שכינה), which in the Kabbalah signifies the manifestation of divinity in feminine aspect. This word derives from the Hebrew verb שכן [*shakan*], 'to settle, inhabit, dwell, in-dwell, abide'. See for example *Exodus* 40:35: "And Moses was not able to enter into the Tent of the Congregation, because the cloud abode [*shakan*] thereon, and the glory of the Lord filled the Tabernacle." The word for 'tabernacle itself, משכן [*mishkan*], 'residence, dwelling place'), is cognate.
>
> I associate and identify the *Shekhinah* both with Gerard Manley Hopkins's conception of *inscape* and *instress*, and with our English words *radiance* and *glory*. The last of these words, incidentally, is cognate with *clear*. At once immanent and transcendental, the *Shekhinah* is often happened upon (discovered, recovered, uncovered) among ephemeral qualities and effects of light and sound that appear to inhere in (settle on, cling to, attach to, belong to) more substantial phenomena.

In his series of masterly books on the Kabbalah, Gershom Scholem tracks the *Shekhinah* through Jewish tradition. He devotes a detailed chapter to the topic, entitled "*Shekhinah*: the Feminine Element in Divinity" (*On the Mystical Shape of the Godhead: Basic Concepts in the Kabbalah,* tr. Jochim Neugroschel, Schocken Books, New York, pp. 140-196), in which he defines the *Shekhinah* primarily as "the presence and hypostatis of God's 'indwelling' in the world" (p. 141), and also identifies the *Shekhinah* with *Malkuth*, the tenth *Sefirah* in the Kabbalah (pp. 43 and 160ff). Elsewhere, he sources the conception of the *Shekhinah* partly in the pre-Christian Gnostic *pleroma* (*Major Trends in Jewish Mysticism*, Thames and Hudson, London, 1955, pp. 229-230), and identifies the *Shekhinah* with the Jewish *Ecclesia* and with the symbolism of the soul (*On the Kabbalah and Its Symbolism*, tr. Ralph Mannheim, Schocken Books, New York, 1978, pp. 104ff). For a further rich variety of contexts, see Louis Ginzberg, *Legends of the Jews* (vol. 2, The Jewish Publication Society, Philadelphia, 2003, pp. 1398-9).

In *For the Living*, 2011, I identify the *Shekhinah* with 'The Rose of Sharon', pp. 57-61. See also the next note.

'True to your absence, glory', p. 5

To honour and remember Jacques Derrida, 1930–2004.

On 'glory', see the previous note and its references, and, for further explorations, the three statements on 'poetry and glory' in *Imagems*, Shearsman Books, Bristol, 2013.

'Radiance palpable, p. 6

In memory of Ilias Layios, 1958–2005.

'This scintillating night', p. 7

For Michael and Mary Rowan-Robinson.

The sestet echoes and responds to Matthew Arnold's poem, 'Dover Beach'. The poem is also a response to Pascal's statement: "Le silence éternel de ces espaces infinis m'effraie." ("The eternal silence of these infinite spaces frightens me.") *Pensées*, 206.

BITTER LOVING, p. 9

Title from Edna St. Vincent Millay, " Last year's bitter loving must remain…", 'Sonnet II', *Poems*, Martin Secker, London, 1929, p. 43.

'First kiss', p. 15

Acknowledgement to Kay Young, *Imagining Minds*, chapter 2 on Jane Austen, entitled 'You Pierce My Soul', Ohio State University Press, Columbus, 2010, pp. 51-67.

'You', p. 15

Acknowledgement to Julia Kristeva: "...An otherness merely touched upon, that already moves away", *Strangers to Ourselves*, tr. Leon S. Roudiez, Columbia University Press, New York, 1991, p. 3.

IDENTITIES, pp. 17–23

To honour Zygmunt Bauman.

'Anybody's guess', p. 19

Acknowledgement to Anthony Barnett: "...not anyone's, anybody's", *Antonyms & Others*, A • B, Lewes, 2012, p. 26.

'Hence into suchness', p. 21

Acknowledgement to Charles Baudelaire: "Adieu donc, chants de cuivre". See 'Le goût du néant', *Fleurs du mal*, 1857.

ON SYNCHRONICITY, pp. 25–31

For Roderick Main.

'When things fit', p. 28

To honour Michael Polanyi, 1891–1976, and Thomas Kuhn, 1922–1996.

'After eternity: a dialogue', p. 31, and 'Give Time', p. 35.

For Catherine Ng.

'Me from the future', p. 37

For Antonio Domínguez Rey.

'Fall on my heels', p. 38

The earliest-written poem in this book, composed in Thebes, Greece, 1967.

'I dreamed I slept', p. 39

In memory of Felicia Burns, née Jacob, 1948–2004.

'NOTNESS', pp. 49–55

"[F]or Augustine, creation exhibits a perfect order or beauty, albeit in its own restricted degree, and the nothingness intrinsic to creation on its own is a necessary part of this order." Catherine Pickstock, 'The

Musical Imperative', *Angelaki, journal of the theoretical humanities*, 3/1, 1998, p. 10.

'Bogomil', p. 53

For Francis R. Jones.

The etymology of the title, from several South Slavonic languages, is *Bog* ('God') and *milost* ('kindness, gentleness, sweetness'). The Bogomils were members of a Manichæan sect which originated in tenth-century Bulgaria. Their dualistic beliefs contained underlying elements of Gnosticism, Zoroastrianism and Mithraism. Members of the sect were systematically persecuted by the Roman and Byzantine empires and by Bulgarian and Serbian dynasties. One theory is that when the Turks overran the Balkan Christian States in the fifteenth century, the Bogomils of Bosnia rapidly converted to Islam. Bogomilism is shrouded in mystery.

'Now', pp. 57–63

For Catherine Pickstock and Robin Kirkpatrick.

'Concerning music', p. 62

Acknowledgement to Catherine Pickstock for a comment on the musical theory of Lacoue-Labarthe: "[T]here can be no notion here of finding one's proper place in time." *op. cit.* p. 14.

'Here is no mourning', p. 63

Acknowledgement to Catherine Pickstock for a comment on postmodern musical theory: "It is mourning for what has never been; it is the attempt of every note or character-type agonistically to oust its predecessor." ibid. *p. 22.*

'Twiceness', pp. 65–71

For Catherine Pickstock.

'David', p. 68

For Carl Schmidt.

Adam Kadmon: Kabbalistic title for the first man, conceived as a representation or microcosm of the power of the entire universe.

'Text and intertext', p. 70

For Norman Finkelstein.

Triggered by a passage in his *Lyrical Interference, Essays on Poetics*, quoting Charles Olson's poem, 'As the Dead Prey Upon Us'. Spuyten Duyvil, New York, 2003, p. 108.

Midrashim (plural of Hebrew *midrash* מדרש). A term combining the meanings of 'exegesis of, commentary on, and inquiry into the meaning of a text', as used by Talmudic scholars in interpreting the Bible and the Law. Each *midrash* is, of course, itself a new text, so the process of commentary is endless.

'Ground', p. 71
For Sebastian Barker, 1946-2014.

'Walking', p. 71
To honour and remember Gerard Manley Hopkins, 1844–1889, and for Antoine Simon.

'FOR AN UNBORN CHILD', pp. 73–77
Homage to James Burns Singer, 1928–1964.

A response to his sequence 'Sonnets to a Dying Man', *The Collected Poems of James Burns Singer*, Secker and Warburg, London, 1970, pp. 62-85.

'These subtle seasons', p. 75
To honour and remember Emmanuel Lévinas, 1906–1995.

'The ghost of the nineteenth century', p. 82
For Angela Leighton.

Lightning Source UK Ltd.
Milton Keynes UK
UKOW02f1126290115

245347UK00002B/24/P